Time is Life
Chapter 1: First steps

Fabrice Blancher

Legal Notices

All rights reserved: No parts of this book may be reproduced or stored in a retrieval system or transmitted in any form or by any electronic, mechanical, photocopying, recording, or otherwise, without the written permission of the publisher.

Liability: This book strives to provide accurate and up-to-date information. However, it cannot guarantee the provided information's accuracy, completeness, or relevance. As a user, you assume full responsibility for using this book and its contents. The author cannot be held responsible for any direct or indirect damages, loss of income, loss of business, or any other harm incurred by the buyer resulting from using the book.

Heartfelt thanks to:

My grandpa Charles, my parents & grandparents, my sister Olivia, Marine Blancher, Nicolas Carteron, Mathieu Mendel, Brinda Venkaya Reichert, Sedley Assonne, Léo Alamelou, Robert Comarmond, Édouard Burgeat, Yahya Kaci, and my wife for her patience and precious help.

Precious dedication:

I would like to thank all the people I have met throughout my Life. Whether short or long-term encounters, you all brought me insights, joys, laughter, and those moments of Life allowed me to step forward, learn, and grow. Today, I begin a new stage of my Life. You are all part of this Life. Hence, I would like to shout a big thank you once again.
You are all in my heart.

Fabrice Blancher
Contact : fabrice.b@timeislife.org

CONTENTS

About the author 4
PROLOGUE 6
1 13
   INTRODUCTION 13
2 18
   MY GRANDFATHER 18
   MY HERO 18
      I - FIRST PART 20
      II - SECOND PART 26
3 31
   FIRST RULES OF LIFE 31
      I - FOOD 31
      II - WATER 34
      III - NATURE 35
      IV - GOOD DEED 38
      V - SMILE 41
      VI - LAUGH 43
4 45
   THE CHILD'S OUTLOOK 45
      I - DISCOVERIES 45
      II - MISTAKES 48
      III - LEARNING 50
      IV - SUCCESS 52
5 57
   EDUCATION 57
      I - THE SQUARE BASE 57
      II - FUNDAMENTAL PRECEPTS 59
6 66
   ILLNESS AND HEALING 66
7 69
   SCHOOL AND STUDIES 69
      I - SCHOOL 69
      II - UNIFORM 71
      III - ACADEMIC BACKGROUND 72
8 77
   SPORT 77
9 82
   SCOUTS 82
10 90
   TIME IS LIFE 90
11 93
   EPILOGUE 93

About the author

Fabrice is a globe trotter, self-taught, passionate about discoveries, and has a Life full of encounters and experiences.

He left France in 2011 at 32, with 1,500 euros in his pocket, intended to live on another continent. For the 13 years afterward, he only spent five months in France. During this period, he has engaged with people from more than fifty countries, further enriching his knowledge and vision of Life.

After another year of significant changes, he begins writing his autobiography. To celebrate his 45th birthday, he published his first book based on the first part of his Life.
A book based on Life itself: how to appreciate Life at its true value, in harmony with the world around us, respecting different cultures, and living in peace.

A book filled with real-Life events and personal quotes. It is a book full of anecdotes and testimonies of people from all walks of Life who oriented and guided him toward an optimistic vision of Life. Just to point out that this view of Life has no terrestrial borders.

This book is a tribute to
all these wonderful people and a hymn to Life.

*I'm a Life lover.
I love social and cultural differences.
I try to understand and incorporate them.
I learned to be very open-minded
with a great capacity for adaptation.
I love discovering the world around me.*

*I'm just an open door pointing a way. If people can
take one step on that path, I'll be happy.*

*Let's always remember that
Time is Life,
thus, let's hurry to take full advantage of it
in Respect and Peace.*

My Life will be my message.

PROLOGUE

Hello everyone,

I'm not a writer, however, I decided to start writing this book to share the experiences and knowledge that made me the man I am today. I would like to retrace my journey and my adventures for all my family and friends scattered around the world, as well as for all the people who will be interested in discovering my personal and spiritual development, my intellectual and human journey, and my path of Life.

I want to share my thirst for Life, my cheerful, optimistic, and somewhat utopian world vision through my education from family and school, my evolution, my successes, my failures, my practical experiences, and my authentic stories of Life.

Moreover, I would like to show you that in Life, with courage, patience, perseverance, and resilience, we can achieve all our dreams, even the craziest ones.

- ❖ Courage allows us to overcome difficulties and not retreat in front of adversity. It drives us to face fear or danger without getting discouraged and empowers us with the strength to defend what we believe in.

- ❖ Patience calms us in difficulties. It allows us the necessary time to avoid making decisions in haste and then achieve our goals.

- ❖ Perseverance allows us not to give up in the face of failure and urges us to start again. It will enable us to learn from our mistakes and never abandon our dreams.

- ❖ Resilience allows us to reduce the negative impact of stress on our well-being. It can also stimulate us to develop strong self-esteem and give us the ability to overcome and adapt to challenges.

These four qualities are interdependent. Each of them can help us develop the other. They are essential and valuable because they can help us live a fulfilling and successful Life. They are critical to making our dreams come true.

In reality, our dreams are goals that are sometimes long and challenging to achieve. But remember that nothing is impossible, and everything is possible. To fulfill our dreams, action is the key.

A few quotes illustrate this idea well:

"We all have dreams. Unless you make a move and take the risk, it will always just be a dream."
Peter Bond (Australian business leader)

❖

"Sometimes the smallest step in the right direction ends up being the biggest step of your Life. Tip toe if you must, but take the step."
Naeem Callaway (American entrepreneur)

❖

"If you really want to change your Life, you'll find a way. If you don't, you'll find an excuse."
Jen Sincero (American writer)

❖

"They didn't know it was impossible, so they did it."
Mark Twain (American writer, 1835-1910)

❖

"The only impossible journey is the one you never start."
Tony Robbins (American writer)

❖

In the era of fake news, mass, and social media, Virtual Reality, Artificial Intelligence, capitalization, industrialization, over-production, compulsive consumption, excessive waste, poverty, famine, climate change, air, land, and ocean pollution, deforestation, drought, violence, and wars, *I believe it is good to come back to simple, basic, fundamental and immutable values which could allow us to live in harmony and peace on this small planet Earth.*

These values include:

- Love: loving oneself, others, and nature.
- Respect: respecting ourselves, everyone else, nature, and all Life.
- Compassion: understanding and sympathizing with the pain and grief experienced by others.
- Generosity: sharing time, resources, and talents with others without expecting anything in return.
- Integrity: being honest, sincere, and trustworthy.
- Responsibility: being accountable for our actions and choices.
- Service: being assistance to help others and improve the world.
- Peace: trying to resolve conflicts and create means of peaceful coexistence.
- Sustainability: taking into account the impact of our actions on future generations.
- Gratitude: being grateful for everything we have.

By adopting these values, we can create a better and more peaceful world where all living beings can live in harmony.

❖

❖

Since my childhood, I have always told myself that if I had to write a book, it would be based on events that happened. Because, whether in my Life or in the lives of people I have encountered over the years, there are infinite incredible stories in front of our eyes.

Often, the most memorable films portray events based on true stories that appeared in "real" Life. So, I told myself that inventing or imagining anything would be pointless.

André Bercoff, a French-Lebanese journalist, declared: "I do not write to write nothing," implying that I do not speak to say nothing; that is to say, I would like to convey a message through my words.

As the chapters unfold, I will reveal how I changed my Life. Step by step, I will tell you my personal stories, which are all linked in time. You will discover the experiences that made me evolve and grow, and ultimately led me to make this big decision:

***Leaving France to live on another continent
and settling there permanently.***

❖

By sharing my experiences and those of the people I have met throughout my Life, I expect to inspire you by showing you that anything is possible.

I hope my story will touch your heart and make you realize that we have the power to change our lives, live happily in harmony, and achieve our dreams above all. Through my story, I hope you can find the strength to continue or begin your own journey in Life.

❖

❖

Yes, now is a difficult time for dreamers,
and yet, Georges Bernanos (French writer, 1888-1948) said:
"If I started my Life again, I would try to make my dreams even bigger
because Life is infinitely more beautiful and bigger than I had believed,
even in dreams."

My friend Bénédicte pointed out to me:
"To make our dreams come true,
sometimes, the most complicated thing is identifying them.
We are so locked into limited beliefs by education and society
that most of our dreams are forgotten."

I answered her:
"The first dream we all have is very simple: Being happy in our lives,
in harmony with ourselves and our surroundings."

*Through this book, I intend to share my perception of happiness
and the simple principles to base on to create,
develop, and maintain deep and lasting fulfillment.*

❖

*Life is beautiful. Life is precious.
Life is short. Time flies.
Time is Life, so let's make the most of it
in Respect and Peace.
Let's make our Life a dream, then bring our dreams to Life.*

❖

"I have a dream."
"So even though we face the difficulties of today and tomorrow,
I still have a dream.

I have a dream that all men, whatever their origins,
would be guaranteed the unalienable rights of Life,
liberty and the pursuit of happiness.
I have a dream that all men are created equal and will be able
to sit down together at the table of brotherhood.
I have a dream that my four little children will one day
live in a nation where they will not be judged will not be judged by
the color of their skin but by the content of their character.
I have a dream that all states sweltering with the heat
of injustice and oppression will be transformed into
an oasis of freedom and justice.

I have a dream that one day every valley shall be exalted,
every hill and mountain shall be made low, the rough places
will be made plain, and the crooked places will be made straight."

Excerpt from "I have a dream." a speech by
Martin Luther King Jr. (American minister, 1929-1968)
delivered on August 28, 1963.

*"Human is always the same:
the systems he creates are always
imperfect, and all the more imperfect for
his self-confidence."*

"Something has to change here."

– Pope John Paul II –

1
INTRODUCTION

Since childhood, every morning, I open my eyes when I wake up, and I am happy. I am so glad because I am breathing and lucky to be still alive. It's another day that Life has given me, a new one opening up for me, and I want to make the most of it.

No one knows how or when our Time will come. Therefore, until my last breath, I want to appreciate, as much as possible, the beautiful treasures that Life brings me so that I have no regrets when my Life ends.

My first inspiration will be a story my father told me when I was very young, marking me ever since. It's a philosophy of Life, an anthem to Life.

It's the story of a man who had cancer with an incurable tumor on the cervical spine. His doctor gave him only six months to live.

The man was initially devastated by the fear of dying, yet decided to make the most of his last days and fulfill his dream of traveling. A dream he had never been able to realize until then, being too busy with his work, his worries, and his daily Life. Hence he determined to sell his possessions and discover the world.

Three months passed by, and he was fine to travel. Then, another three months passed by, and still, he continued to travel onwards without feeling any effects of the illness that had been consuming him. Furthermore, after ten months, still alive, he decided to return to see his doctor to examine his cancer.

When the doctor saw his patient return with a big smile and in good health, he thought he saw a ghost and said to him in shock: "You're alive! How is that possible?" He found it hard to believe that the patient was still alive. The man replied with a question: "Do you want to know what I've been doing these past months?" But the doctor, on the contrary, not wanting to know by what magic or sorcery he could still be standing, asked him to leave and closed the door in his face.

Because for him, a Cartesian man who believes solely in fundamental principles and scientifically verifiable facts, not in myths or superstitions, there was no concrete and plausible explanation for what was happening.

In the end, after an examination at another doctor's surgery, it turned out that the cancerous tumor had completely reabsorbed and miraculously disappeared. He had healed himself by realizing his dream, changing his thinking, eliminating daily stresses, and enjoying his Life to the fullest. He discovered the power of the mind by meeting a yogi on a trip. He became a lecturer on the subject. He has also written several books and created "The Brofman Foundation for the Advancement of Healing." His terminal illness was diagnosed in 1975. Martin Brofman, his real name, ultimately lived until 2014.

His story is full of hope and infinite possibility.
It is an inspiration to us all. It shows us that
we could change our lives by making our dreams come true.

My mum used to say to me:
"We have to learn to live on our feet,"
quoting Jacques Brel (Belgian singer, 1929-1978):
"We have to live on our feet and on the move."

❖

French singer Patrick Hernandez describes this idea with his worldwide hit "Born to be Alive." The refrain, "I was born to be alive, I was born to be free, I was born to be me," is an anthem to Life and joy. Full of energy and optimism, this song encourages us to live our lives without restraint.

A Brazilian writer, Paulo Coelho, symbolized this concept when he drafted his epitaph, his gravestone, with "Paulo Coelho died while he was alive." He explains: "To die alive is to take risks, to do something that could frighten you, but that you might enjoy."

❖

"No one knows what he can do until he tries."
Publilius Syrus (Latin writer, 85 BC-43 BC)

"To innovate is to dare to take risks."
René Lacoste (French tennis player, 1904-1996)

All these words encourage us to make the most of Life and explore all the possibilities. Remember that we can achieve anything if we dare to believe in ourselves, even if it sometimes comes with fear.

❖

As Mark Twain explained:
"The fear of dying is the result of the fear of living.
A person who lives fully is ready to die at any moment."

And Norman Cousins (American writer, 1915-1990) added:
"The tragedy of Life is not death,
but what we allow to die in us while we live."

❖

Even if you're afraid to die, don't be scared to live.

Life is beautiful and precious. We all have our dreams and the power to realize them. However, fear and anxiety can sometimes prevent us from moving forward. At times like these, let's remember that living Life to the fullest is the only way to avoid regret and remorse.

❖

In addition, "we never go as far as when we don't know where we're going." This way of thinking by Christopher Columbus (Italian explorer, 1451-1506) enabled him to discover the Americas in 1492.

This echoes the theme we discussed earlier: to motivate us to be brave enough to pursue our dreams, even if we don't know where they will take us. We can achieve anything if we have the will and strength to work towards our goals.

Idriss Aberkane, a French writer, sums it up perfectly when he says: "True Life is true diversity. True diversity is existence; it's the trials of Life, and it's serious. In real Life, you're not defeated until you give up. That's what real Life is all about."

In other words:

"There is only one way to fail:
That is to give up before you've succeeded."
Georges Clémenceau (French politician, 1841-1929)

"Those who give up never win. Those who win never give up."
Napoleon Hill (American author, 1883-1970)

❖

Achieving a Life goal is like building a sandcastle. We work hard to build it, but the waves constantly come and knock it over. However, if we persevere, low tide will eventually arrive. (Inspired by "My Name")

Therefore, let's never give up on our dreams because Life is not a long quiet river. Life is nothing but a series of ups and downs, combined with unpredictable risks. Dreams only come true when we take the risk of realizing them and there is no reward without risk.

In addition: "It's not that we have very little time; it's rather that we waste a lot of it." (Seneca, a Latin philosopher, 4 BC-65 AD). All this reminds us that Life is short, that Life is fleeting, and that we need to make the most of it. With the idea of not wasting Time, because Time passes very quickly, Time cannot be regained, and Time is Life.

❖

Time is Life. Life is about being happy and enjoying every single moment. This can be done simply if we feel peaceful and respect those around us, our environment, and the planet. This way of thinking has guided me throughout my Life.

2
MY GRANDFATHER MY HERO

I love Life; I love to enjoy Life. In my Life, all began with my beloved grandfather, Grandpa Charles, who was my first example. He lived almost 100, and despite his senior age, he continued to discover new things in this world with great curiosity and fascination. He rocked the first steps of my sister and me in our childhood.

As I sat with him for hours, watching him and listening to him, telling me about his long Life, I thought to myself: "Wow, there are so many things to discover and explore in this world that I'll never have enough time to see everything. I could never discover everything, try everything, or experience everything."

I discovered that Life is a perpetual learning process, where every day brings something new to discover and understand as if I knew nothing and those discoveries and knowledge were infinite.

Michel Fugain, a French singer, marked this idea perfectly in his 1969 song "I won't have time " ("Je n'aurai pas le temps"):
"Even by running, faster than the wind, faster than time, even by flying, I will not have time to visit all the immensity of such a large universe. Even in a hundred years, I won't have time to do everything. I open my heart wide. I love it with all my eyes. It's too little for so many hearts and so many flowers. Thousands of days are far too short. And to love, as we should love, when we truly love, even in a hundred years, I will not have time."

❖

❖

Charles was not just a living memory,
he was also a living legend.

"When someone you love becomes a memory,
his memory becomes a treasure."

My grandpa Charles had a very long Life,
so his story will unfold in two parts.
The following is his Life.

I - FIRST PART

It all began on 17 April 1909, with the union of his parents, Eugène and Louise.

Charles Gasiglia was born on February 18, 1912, in Nice, south of France. In those days, babies were born at home under the watchful eye of a midwife.

He lived at number 17 Assalit Street, in a flat with his parents and two brothers, Louis and Honoré. It was a flat that he lived in for most of his Life until the age of 95.

Back in 1918, running water took a lot of work to come by on the 6th floor. So he had to fetch water buckets from the minor public fountain on the ground floor of the building, obviously without an elevator.

Here is the first little anecdote. Eighty years later, in 1997, when the city hall removed the fountain, which caused more trouble for the locals, as the result he initiated a petition to have it reinstalled. He collected around 500 signatures from the residents and shopkeepers in the area and wrote to the mayor at the time, Jacques Peyrat.

Here is the transcript of his letter, "Requiem for a Fountain."

"Dear Sir,"

"I was stunned this morning when I came downstairs from my house on the corner of Assalit Street and Miron Street. A centenarian has been killed, or should I say made to disappear. I mean the fountain that had always been standing at the foot of the building where I was born. Yet, it wasn't sick or tired but did a lot of good deeds.

If I were to tell you that when I was growing up in the 1920s, the water couldn't reach the 6th floor because there wasn't enough pressure. We had to climb down with buckets and bottles to collect water from the fountain without a lift.

It's still beneficial today. Sometimes, a poor homeless person, unable to get into a café, quenches his thirst at the pump and takes the opportunity to refresh his face. And he takes his plastic bottle with him, filled with this beneficial water.

Similarly, many of the dogs in Nice come to lap up the water: you should have seen how happy they are in summer. The local shopkeepers also used it to throw in a bucket of water to keep the area clean because all these shops are over 100 years old, and many don't have water on site.

I wonder who knows whether our greatest French poet, Lamartine, would have written his masterpiece "The Lake" if he had been away from his beloved lake? Twenty-five meters further on, the fountain would have been in Lamartine Street!

Similarly, if it hadn't been for a spring, would our admirable Provençal poet Marcel Pagnol have created his masterpiece "Manon des Sources"?

Lastly, would the poet Petrarch have written so dreamily if he hadn't gone to court with his beloved fiancée, Laure de Noves, by the Vaucluse Fountain?

In conclusion, why would you remove a sign of Life at a time when many communes in France are paying tribute to water and fountains? Because Water is Life! If one day, water disappeared from the planet, Life would also come to an end. No, we beg you: give us back our FOUNTAIN!"

The mayor replied as soon as possible, it goes:

"Dear Sir,"

"I read your fascinating letter in which you lament with emotion the removal of a fountain installed in front of the building where you were born.

The pleasure of turning the crank on the fountain and drinking from the tap to quench our thirst on summer days when, as children, we finished school, is still too vivid in my mind for me not to share your regret.

The passage of time inevitably leads to changes in the town we knew from fifty years ago. However, I would ask the relevant department to look into remedying this disappearance, which deprived the people of Nice of a historical element."

Yours sincerely, Jacques Peyrat, Deputy Mayor of Nice.

The fountain was eventually reinstalled in the same place, and there was even a tiny inauguration with all the locals to celebrate its return in the presence of the mayor and, of course, my grandpa Charles.

❖

In addition to that, until 1924, when Charles was 12, the building had no gas or electricity. He used candles and gasoline lamps for light.

There was no refrigerator, so he used a large cupboard as an icebox, filled with blocks of ice delivered every morning.

Likewise, there was no washing machine either. A washerwoman, Miss Surla, came every week with her cart to collect the laundry. She would wash the clothes in a stream called "le Magnan" in the Madeleine Valley, west of Nice, and bring them back the following week.

Obviously, there were no telephones or television, and the music was recorded on metal discs played by the forerunner of the vinyl record player, the "Symphonion," a manual music box from the 1880s.

Throughout his Life, Charles's landmark was Notre-Dame church on Jean Médecin Avenue. He often rang the bells so heavily that they threw him into the air.

Jean Médecin Avenue was his playground. It used to be called Station Avenue, then, after the 14-18 War, Victory Avenue, before taking its definitive name. The tram passed in front of his house so he could get on and off as he went.

In 1919, at 7, he started to study at Notre Dame, the only school he attended, from the 7th to the highest 1st grade. There, he passed his school-leaving certificate in 1925 at 13 years old.

On top of that, he was a high-level sportsman. He took part in several sports, including gymnastics and basketball. He was nicknamed the mosquito because of his small size. He couldn't touch the hoop in basketball, but in defense, he was unstoppable and had an incredible game vision. He was also the Côte d'Azur volleyball champion.

He even participated in the "Tour de France" amateur cycling race in 1950. One day apart, the participants followed the same route as the official race for professional cyclists.

I am happy to share that one of his adventures appeared in the newspaper.

"Touring cyclist Charles Gasiglia was not spared. According to his statements, he had set off with the sole aim of taking a budget holiday and touring our beautiful country of France.

From the very first day, like all the other people from the Côte d'Azur, he fell victim to a rule that was too strict. They had drawn up their timetable based on the distance to be covered at an average of 22 km per hour. But because of a last-minute change that shortened the route by a few kilometers, they arrived at the finish of the first stage nine minutes ahead of schedule and were awarded 27 penalty points.

Thus, handicapped from the very first stage, Charles had only one goal left: to complete his Tour de France on time and make the most of everything he could admire along the way.

Unfortunately for him, during the "Vannes-Dinant" stage, at "Mur-de-Bretagne," to be precise, he was the victim of a crash caused by a dog that had thrown itself into the peloton. Picked up unconscious by his comrades, he was hastily treated on the spot and then in the nearest village. A doctor attended to him, and despite severe intercostal and right shoulder pains, he courageously resumed his journey.

However, all this wasted time prevented him from passing two secret controls hidden along the road on time. And even though he had come back very well, having completed this stage on time, the organizers were inflexible that he should be eliminated, which, in our opinion, is simply inhuman.

But Charles Gasiglia didn't want to consider himself defeated, and, overcoming his suffering, he continued the race. He finished with his comrades at the "Champs-Élysées" in Paris."

An example of courage and bravery.

❖

On the side, I also want to share a personal story that truly embodies this mindset. When I was younger, I used to run marathons.

In one particular race, 600 runners were packed at the starting line. As the starting whistle blew, marking the beginning of the race, everyone surged forward in a massive human wave.

Amidst this burst of energy, someone tripped me, causing me to fall hard, gashing both knees and getting trampled by fellow runners. Despite the pain and bloodied knees, I refused to admit defeat or give up.

With courage, I picked myself up and resumed the race from the very back. Given the marathon's lengthy distance, stretching across numerous kilometers, I gradually made up for lost time and astonishingly finished in 5th place. This act of perseverance and resilience was a legacy inherited from my grandfather.

Then, in 1940, at 28, Charles was recruited into the army for the Second World War and posted to the hills above Nice in the neutral zone. He initially joined the 157th Foot Artillery Regiment. Then, he was appointed chief brigadier and took charge of the regiment's quartermaster's office.

On his return from the army, Charles, a handsome young man, met Madeleine Palazzoli, who was to become his wife. The wedding took place at the Vallon Obscur church. My mother was born in their union. The four of them lived in the same small two-room flat with his mother, wife, and daughter, and they didn't have much money.

Despite this, he adopted Florent, the son of his wife's brother, who had five children and very little means of support after the war. The five of them lived together for several years, crowded but happy. Florent has become like a brother to my mother.

After the war, in 1947, not finding work in France, he went to work in Algeria, where he was employed as a fabric cutter. His wife couldn't join him as she had to take care of the children, so he decided in 1948 to return to France and began working as a tailor.

In 1951, he bought a shop at number 7 Maréchal Joffre Street, which became his workshop and where he remained for 34 years, until 31 December 1985. Since then, he remained an artisan tailor and was awarded the Gold Medal for Craftsmanship in 1968.

He even created the uniform and dressed the entire Nice fire brigade in a distant era when craftsmen did everything by hand and not by machines.

All his Life, he only wore clothes he made himself. Always a class outfit, dressed in a suit and tie, he only took the tie off once a year, during the week of 15 August, which, in his words, was the hottest week of the year.

Meanwhile, in 1954, he became one of the founding members of A.S.C.A., Côte d'Azur First Aid Association (Association des Secouristes de la Côte d'Azur), which teaches and practices Life-saving first aid. This association is still active today.

Charles was the happiest man in the world with his wife, Mado (Madeleine). Unfortunately, she died at fifty-eight years old. I never got to meet my grandmother. However, Papi Charles never stopped loving her and thinking about her. He remained single for almost forty years. He kept his wedding ring on his finger until the last few days and waited to see her again in heaven. The most beautiful love.

The first part of my grandpa Charles' Life was full of experiences.
The second half of his Life will be just as rich.

II - SECOND PART

Even after my grandfather stopped working at 73 years old, he continued many activities. He first helped in the secretariat in my father's office for four years.

On the side, for almost 3/4 of a century, he was the unshakeable pillar of the famous association of local people of Nice, "Niçois," "Nissarte," known as "l'Estocaficada." The name comes from a dish from Nice called "stockfish" or "estocafic," made from dried cod.

Along with the association, he attended the most important opening ceremonies, weddings, and funerals in Nice. Also, to keep Nice's culinary traditions alive, once a month, the participants would get together for huge buffets featuring "estocafic," "Niçoise" stew, "Niçoise" salad, "socca" (baked chickpea flour), "farcis" (vegetables stuffed with meat), "pissaladière" (pizza with onions, herring, and black olives), flower fritters zucchini and chard pie.

These parties could last several hours, and they liked to sing the Nice anthem, "Nissa La Bella," to close the meeting. In 1995, they celebrated their 90th anniversary with a pantagruelian menu.

Besides, he was an eternal member of the official Nice choir of the Notre Dame church, "Nikaïachor," made up of 30 or 40 singers, and was a baritone singer. They even went to sing for Pope John Paul II in the church of San Ignacio in Roma (Italia)
in 1992.

In 1997, he was present with his former classmates on the last day before the demolition of his old school, Notre Dame. Glowing like an angel among the schoolchildren, he remained as young and smiley as they were.

He also became an extra actor at the "La Victorine" film studios. He even got to appear in a film. On the side, he also acted in a small play, the role of the witch in Snow White, to amuse the children.

Moreover, he was also involved in organizing the famous Nice International Triathlon as a volunteer for several years.

He could be a guitarist, a cook, a dancer, a player, a charmer, a gourmand. He was even in the mafia, one of the oldest godfathers, obviously for fun.

At 92, he passed his school-leaving certificate again, obtained 79 years earlier, which earned him an article in the town newspaper.

As an assistant to the deputy mayor at the wedding of Eric et Corinne, the daughter of his adopted son Florent; he was even mayor of Nice for a few minutes.

As a tailor for years, he had been collecting fabrics and sewing threads and buttons. With these, he continued to create clothes, hats, blankets, and cushions to give to his family and friends. He became the king of patchwork, creating one-off handmade art pieces such as those below.

He was always present at family celebrations like Christmas or birthdays, and for his 90th birthday, thanks to a beautiful idea from my mum, I made him a Golden book, a book of hours, from which I took most of his stories.

I enjoyed it; sometimes, it was hard not to cry during the making because my grandpa Charles's Life was so fascinating, and the stories were full of feelings and memories.

❖

All his family and long-standing friends were able to write
a message in his Golden book. Here is the summary.

"For a wonderful dad, grandpa, and friend."

"Polyphony is an art that brings beauty to people, improves them, opens them up, and makes them available to others. Undoubtedly, Charles, you had benefited from the advantages César Geoffrey discovered when he devoted his Life to teaching polyphony,

Charles is a living memory. He is a genuine man with a big heart, a good listener, and always ready to help, both in his work and for his family and friends.

He makes the most of his Life, showing kindness, generosity, accessibility, friendliness, humor, and courage, especially in difficult times. Always smiling to the very end of his Life."

After enjoying nine additional years of happiness,
my grandpa Charles sadly passed away on February 5, 2011,
just one week before celebrating his 99th birthday.

Here's the secret of his longevity:

Throughout his Life, he never stopped caring
for his body and mind while having a great open mindset.

• **In terms of food:** He had a healthy, simple, and balanced diet. He always shopped in his street, where most shopkeepers were his friends. He never went to a supermarket; he found everything in his neighborhood. He bought fresh products and food straight from the gardens or local farms. His breakfast, for example, consisted of fruit, French toast, and five varieties of cereal, all accompanied by a large pot of coffee.

• **In terms of physique:** He played a lot of sports like my paternal grandfather, Grandpa Maurice, who played tennis until he was 82 and passed away at 95.

Papi Charles also always rode a "Solex," a famous motorbike he had to pedal uphill. To feel at ease and free, he was always without a helmet. He had obtained an exceptional written exemption from his doctor to be presented to the police in the event of a check-up, forbidding him to wear a helmet.

When the lift finally appeared, which was a revolution then, he continued to take the stairs up the six flights to keep fit. He even enjoyed running upstairs to get in front of his next-door neighbors so that he could open the door of the lift for them.

• **In terms of mind:** Since he never had a television, he exercised his brain and mind by reading a lot and doing crosswords. He was a maestro. Also, he would always cut out interesting newspaper articles for us to read.

In brief, he was also very open-minded, wore his heart on his sleeve, and was altruistic. The definitions of these two character traits sum up his entire personality.

- **Wear his heart on his sleeve:** "Being open, frank, unconcealed, and generous."
- **Altruistic/Selflessness:** "Willing to look after others and take an interest in them."

Sharing, exchanging, and understanding others were his primary qualities. He always offered discounts to his customers in need and often accepted credit, which he sometimes found difficult to get back.

On top of that, he liked to give small gifts to everyone, always telling me that it's not the size or value of the gift that matters; "it's the good intention that counts." What matters most is the gesture or the thoughtfulness towards the other person.

All these are to explain that even though he only had one wife, lived in one flat, never owned a television, a computer, or a mobile phone, never had a driver's license, and never really left his hometown, my grandpa Charles had many experiences in his Life.

My grandfather was an incredible person, a wonderful and rare kind who left a long-lasting impression on me. Everything he achieved and his vision of Life made him the person I admire and love the most.

Through his rich Life and mentality, he is a role model for everyone to follow, for all present and future generations.

He was and will remain my hero forever.
My grandpa Charles, I love you for Life.

3
FIRST RULES OF LIFE

In my childhood, my grandpa Charles has imparted the fundamental Life principles to me, simple yet profoundly significant truths about Life. These basic rules, though straightforward, are essential to living in harmony on this little planet Earth.

I - FOOD

From my earliest memories, my grandfather made me aware of the great fortune I had to have daily food and water. We must be grateful for what Life offers us. He taught me that there is an infinite variety of foods in this world; thus, we should train ourselves to eat everything.

He also explained that in my existence, learned in his time of war, I might not always have the luxury of choosing my food. Therefore, I had to learn to love and at least be content with as many different foods as possible, thereby training my palate to accept various tastes, varieties, and spices and, in doing so, broadening my mind.

Love is a feeling; it takes place in the mind and is all about mentality. We can learn to appreciate and love all things. This also depends on the education we receive from our family. The more our parents expose us to, the more open our minds could be to all sorts of differences. But that depends mainly on ourselves and our approach to Life.

"When we don't have what we love, we have to love what we have." – Serge Gainsbourg (French singer, 1928-1991)

❖

Grandpa Charles also impressed upon me the importance of always finishing my plate. We must not waste or throw away food, especially considering that if we ever faced scarcity, we would fight over mere crumbs. More importantly, we should remember all the people and children around the world who, even in our so-called "modern" era, suffer from malnutrition and famine.

My sister and I were raised with a strict yet fair upbringing; it was crucial not to waste. If I didn't finish my meal at dinner, I couldn't leave the table, or I had to eat it for breakfast the following day.

I've never understood certain societal norms, such as the so-called good manners in restaurants of leaving some food on your plate to indicate you've had enough or that the meal was sufficient. Or decorating plates with vegetables or salad that no one eats. In some countries, this is a senseless and incomprehensible waste.

My grandfather and I loved finishing our plates by licking up to the last crumb, even if it was against my parents' rules.

❖

It's worth noting that we could feed nearly twice the global population had it not been for the impartial distribution of the planet's food resources.

According to the World Wildlife Fund (World Wide Fund for Nature - WWF), 40% of produced food is not consumed yearly. 2.5 billion tons of food are thrown away. The surplus from mass food production is either lost or wasted, with 16% of global food lost due to inadequate harvesting, handling, storage, and transportation. Restaurants discard 37%, and also consumers waste 47%. These numbers are sadly shocking.

Currently, according to the United Nations, over three billion people lack access to nutritious food, while nearly two billion suffer from overweight or obesity. According to the United Nations, about 25,000 people, including more than 10,000 children, die from hunger each day. Hunger is the leading cause of death worldwide each year, which is incomprehensible and unacceptable.

❖

*The surplus from mass production
could be used more effectively.
Hence, I must repeat, to save humanity and the planet,
let us finish our plates and never waste food.*

❖

According to Pierre Rabhi (French writer, 1938-2021):
"Agriculture should be the first health activity.
The farmer must precede the doctor."

❖

Permaculture – a mode of agriculture based on the principles of sustainable development, intended to respect biodiversity and humans, consisting of imitating the functioning of natural ecosystems (source Larousse) – ***is an advantageous solution.***

❖❖❖

II - WATER

Following the previous section on food, my grandfather Charles also taught me not to waste water, which is equally critical, as countless individuals worldwide lack access to water or do not have running water.

Currently, according to the United Nations and the World Health Organization, over two billion people globally lack access to safe drinking water, and 3.6 billion people use inadequate water sanitation services.

Jean-Paul Augereau created the Safe Water Cube Fountain in 2015, entirely mechanical, enabling any type of water to be recycled and drinkable. 340 fountains in 20 countries worldwide have been installed, benefiting 250,000 people.

We must save water and not "use it unnecessarily."
For instance, we should take shorter showers, regularly turn off taps while brushing teeth or washing dishes, reduce toilet flush volumes, run washing machines on eco mode with full loads, promptly repair water leaks, and collect rainwater for watering plants or gardens.

It's essential to recognize that water is a scarce resource, and for many countries, it is more valuable than gold. Thus, let's not waste water.

The same principle applies to electricity, heating, or air conditioning. Turning off lights and electronic devices when leaving a room saves and reduces our planet's energy consumption.

I must repeat: to save the Planet, let's save water.

❖❖

III - NATURE

With the same respect for the planet in mind, my grandfather taught me never to litter, especially not in nature. It would make my grandpa sad to see all this trash everywhere. Therefore, I tend to clean them up every time I see them.

Let's consider the decomposition times of common waste in the environment. The figures vary based on conditions: cigarette butts and chewing gum take 1 to 5 years, plastic straws take 100 to 200 years, metal cans take 50 to 500 years, plastic bottles take 400 to 1,000 years, and glass bottles take 4,000 to 1,000,000 years.

Informative fact: according to the association "Save 4 Planet," annually, 4.3 trillion cigarette butts are discarded on the ground or directly into the water, equating to nearly 12 billion per day. A single cigarette butt can pollute up to 500 liters of water, rendering it unfit for consumption.

"Don't be a tosser! If it's not in the bin, it's on you."

Each year, the world produces 460 million tons of plastic, of which only 9% is recycled and 12% is incinerated. The remaining plastic pollutes the environment or ends up in landfills and dumps. (Source TF1 info)

Annually, 5 to 13 million tons of plastics are dumped into the oceans, leading to what is known as the 7th continent—an immense floating garbage patch in the North Pacific Ocean, about one-third of the United States or six times the size of France. This pollution also affects the South Pacific Ocean, the North and South Atlantic Oceans, the Indian Ocean, and the Mediterranean Sea.

❖

A project of the Environmental Protection Authority
of New South Wales - Australia: waste less, recycle more,
initiative funded by the waste levy. A few figures:

- 80% of marine debris come from land-based sources.
- By 2050, there will be more plastic, by weight, in the oceans than fish.
- It's estimated that we consume the equivalent of a credit card's worth of plastic every week!

Several non-governmental organizations work tirelessly
to protect the environment and oceans:

Algalita	Bloom	Cetasea	Greenpeace
An Ocean of Life	Blue Ocean Watch	Expedition 7th Continent	Ocean Cleanup
Ocean No Plastic	One Tree Planted	Plastic Odyssey	Project Rescue Ocean
Longitude 181	Oceana	NRDC	Save 4 Planet
Sea Cleaners	Sea Shepherd	Surfrider	Tara Ocean
Take3 for the sea	Water Family	Wings of the Ocean	WWF

And many others. Feel free to support these organizations
through volunteering or any form of contribution.

This pollution impacts all aspects of the environment – plant,
animal, mineral, and eventually human. Greenpeace aptly stated,
"What's scarier than an ocean with sharks?
An ocean without sharks."

In Japan, one of the cleanest countries in the world, recycling is paramount. 85% of plastic bottles are recycled, aiming for 100% by 2030. Kamikatsu, a pioneering zero-waste town, holds the record with 34 to 45 selective waste categories, achieving an 80% recycling rate. Residents must sort their waste at home and bring it to the recycling center, which has replaced the incineration plant.

❖

Typically, waste is separated into six categories:
Metal, electronics, plastic, glass, paper, and organic.
Recycling waste is of utmost importance to save the planet.
Let's recycle today for a better tomorrow.

❖

As Mahatma Gandhi (Indian lawyer, 1869-1948) said:
"What we are doing to the world's forests is nothing but a mirror reflection of what we are doing to ourselves and one another."

❖

Considering others and being mindful of our surroundings
means to be open to the world.
Thus, whenever we encounter litter in nature, forests, or beaches, let's pick it up and throw it in the garbage bin.

*Remember, each of our actions has an impact,
not only on our immediate surroundings and environment
but also on the entire planet.*

IV - GOOD DEED

Another fundamental value that my grandpa Charles instilled in me is to be sociable. By its definition, "a sociable person is someone who can live peacefully with others, enjoys the company of others, and is capable of keeping kind human relations."

My grandfather taught me to perform at least one good deed daily to become sociable. Good deeds hold a primary place in sociability.

He always reminded me:
"It's the good intention that counts."
***"What matters most is the gesture or
the attention towards others."***

❖

Pope John Paul II (1920-2005) also declared:
"Doing good does not come naturally."

This means that acting justly and morally can be challenging. Facing injustice, suffering, or others' pain can be difficult. It may also be hard to make personal sacrifices to help others. Despite the difficulties, it's indubitable to do good. It makes us better individuals and contributes to creating a better world.

We must always remember to help and support our fellow beings, that is everyone around us or those we encounter daily.

"See the good in people and help them."
– Mahatma Gandhi –

***Helping people overcome obstacles
brings positive changes to their lives.***

❖

A good deed can be a simple act. Here are a few examples: giving up your seat on the bus or train to priority individuals – seniors, disabled persons, people with heart conditions, mothers with children, or pregnant women – assisting someone in crossing the street, helping someone carry their bags, yielding to pedestrians while driving, giving directions to someone who is lost, donating food to a homeless person, picking up and returning a lost item, assisting a colleague at work, offering water to a thirsty dog, or offering support to someone in need.

Nothing is too small to be done.
Any task or action, no matter how small,
is not too insignificant to be accomplished.

A good deed is a form of civility, courtesy, and politeness crucial in creating and spreading a positive atmosphere around us. Note that, when someone helps us while they are also in difficulty, it's not just help; it's love.

❖

As Buddha (500 BC) said:
"A single word that brings comfort is better
than a hundred useless speeches."

❖

Mahatma Gandhi added:

- "The best way to find ourselves is to lose ourselves in the service of others."
- "A man becomes great as he works for the welfare of his fellow beings."

❖

The Dalai Lama encapsulates this thought by saying:
"We are only visitors on this planet. We are here for ninety or one hundred years at the most. During that period, we must try to do something good, something meaningful in our lives. If you contribute to other people's happiness, you will find the true purpose and the true meaning of Life."

My friend Dorothée Nakache concludes by saying:
"Life is a gift. Sometimes it's hard to see it,
but when someone helps us, it's another gift."

Ultimately, being a good person does not depend on our religion, status, race, color, political views, or culture. Being a good person depends on how we treat others. (Buddhist thought)

"We are not all in the same boat. We are in the same storm.
But some have yachts, some have canoes, and some are drowning.
Just be kind and help whoever you can."
– Damian Barr (Scottish writer) –

We are all on the same planet,
so let's care for and respect each other.

Moreover, it's pretty clear that one good deed daily is not enough. Therefore, let's repeat multiple good deeds and spread good energies worldwide. Imagine if everyone in France or around the world started doing good deeds every day so that the overall atmosphere would be completely transformed for the better.

V - SMILE

My grandfather was exceptionally sociable. He enjoyed meeting new people, sharing laughs, and making jokes with them, always wearing a big smile.

The smile holds an undeniable position in sociability, akin to a good deed. A smile is the foundation of positive human relations. It is a universal language, a distinct message conveying our feelings and emotions at the moment. My father would say, "The eyes are the mirror to the soul, and the smile is one of its best expressions."

There are various types of smiles, such as the complicit, daring, embarrassed, affectionate, even forced smiles, and so on. Yet, the most essential is the welcoming smile that fosters initial contact with new acquaintances. It's an inviting and positive smile, signaling to others that they can confidently approach us.

Victor Borge (Danish-American comedian/pianist, 1909-2000)
captured this notion perfectly by stating:
"A smile is the shortest distance between two people."

The smile is an invitation to communication and exchange.
The power of a smile is so immense that it cannot be measured.

❖

Let me tell you a little story to illustrate this.
The smile is contagious. You catch it like the flu.
When someone smiled at me today, I started to smile, too.
I walked around the corner, and someone saw me smiling.
When he smiled back, I realized I had passed it on to him.
I thought about the smile, and then I recognized its value.
A single smile like mine could go around the Earth.
Now, if you feel a smile starting, don't leave it unnoticed.
Start an epidemic and infect the world.

That's how our light can change the world.

Smiles are infectious and reassuring; they make most people feel at ease, relaxed and prompt them to smile. Everything about smiling is beneficial, not only for our well-being but also for the well-being of others.

A few quotes succinctly convey this thought:

- ❖ "Flowers need sunshine; human beings need smile."
- ❖ "A smile costs less than electricity, but it gives just as much light."
- ❖ "With your smile, you make Life more beautiful." – Thich Nhat Hanh (Vietnamese Buddhist monk, 1926-2022)
- ❖ "We shall never know how much good a simple smile can do." – Mother Teresa (Albanian-Indian Catholic nun, 1910-1997)
- ❖ "A smile is the best makeup a girl can wear." – Marilyn Monroe (American actress, 1926-1962)

The power of a smile is immeasurable, it can emancipate the most introverted people, disarm the strongest, calm the angriest and soothe the most tormented.
Therefore, let's always smile.

VI - LAUGH

Like a smile, laughter is essential in Life as it maintains good mental and physical health.

I remember my childhood with my grandfather, we spent hours laughing together. One of my fondest memories was watching the movie "The Visitors" by Jean-Marie Poiré at the cinema in 1993. We laughed with tears from start to finish. I laughed so hard that I fell off my chair, rolling on the floor with laughter.

Other unforgettable moments were when we watched Bud Spencer and Terence Hill films. With their humor and their funny fight with big slaps, we laughed non-stop.

My grandpa also made me laugh the day cordless phones appeared. He would wave his hand around in intrigued and amused wonder, trying to grasp how a wireless, invisible connection could work.

❖

Is it true to say, "We must laugh for at least 15 minutes a day to stay healthy"? Absolutely! Did you know that laughter positively affects every part of our body?

Laughter boosts the immune system, neuro-hormonal system, respiratory function, sleep quality, mood, intellect, self-esteem, self-confidence, communication with oneself and others, emotional well-being, digestion, energy levels, pain tolerance, memory, muscular system, and cardiovascular system.

*A simple laugh holds remarkable benefits
for physical and mental well-being.*

❖

"Laughter is a dust of joy that makes the heart sneeze."
Sandrine Fillassier (French writer)

That's why it's important to laugh.
A day without laughter is a day wasted.
Life is short, so let's laugh unconditionally
and always remember what made us smile and laugh.

Ultimately, with my grandfather, we lived through simple moments filled with joy and overwhelming happiness sprinkled with kindness and perpetual altruism. All these rules of Life that he taught me from an early age are essential for a world at peace and in harmony. They are as simple as they are important. By applying them every day, we have the power to profoundly transform the planet. It's up to us to realize this.

"If you wanna make the World a better place,
take a look at yourself in the mirror,
and then make a change"
– Michael Jackson –

"If we dream of a better world,
it's up to us to build it,
because the World is US!"
– Frédérique Bedos (Jouranliste française) –

WE ARE THE WORLD,
SO LET'S MAKE THAT CHANGE
AND HEAL THE PLANET!

4
THE CHILD'S OUTLOOK

As you would understand, I hold my grandfather, Charles, in high regard. Another lesson he imprinted on me was his perspective on Life. He matured while retaining a child's heart, viewing Life through a child's outlook, and admiring Life with wonder.

Through the four stages essential to the excellent development of the child – discoveries, errors, learning, and successes – I will describe this vision of Life, which is vital for our growth and personal emancipation.

I - DISCOVERIES

I often say: *"It's essential always to view Life with the child's outlook,"* that innate sense of wonder we possess from birth.

> "Life must be embraced as it comes,
> with a child's joyful smile at dawn."
> Jean-Marie Guyau (French philosopher, 1854-1888)

A child will gradually discover the world around him, a world strewn with novelties that he will seek to decode and understand with an innate curiosity. Anything different from what they already know will attract their attention.

Novelty is intriguing and alluring, possibly frightening, but curiosity drives the child to understand the difference by observing and exploring it.

Approaching cautiously, yet driven by an eagerness to understand, a child might touch and analyze the new object, undeterred by the unknown, believing in the potential value of this discovery.

❖

Childlike curiosity is the basis of intellectual development in children and the driving force behind learning.
Childlike curiosity is one of the finest human qualities.
It lays the groundwork for discovery.

❖

Here's a funny example: I hadn't learned to swim when I was four years old. The first time I saw a pool, I was so excited that I ran and jumped immediately into the water, much to my mother's horror. Bystanders screamed for someone to rescue me, but like a little pup, I instinctively started swimming to the edge, beaming with pride. Often, it's fear and panic that lead to drowning.

Similarly, during family trips, my excitement and curiosity to explore new things was so uncontrollable that I'd dash around, forcing my mother, quite sensibly, to keep me leashed to prevent me from getting lost.

❖

A child is constantly looking for exciting novelties, unburdened by prejudice or preconceived notions of difference, unashamed or unembarrassed. Faced with an obstacle, a child doesn't run away or flee but seeks ways to overcome it.

Interest fades quickly once a child grasps a new discovery, much like a new toy. Once the novelty wears off and the newfound knowledge becomes familiar, their curiosity shifts towards fresh explorations.

❖

As we grow, we gain experience, maturity, and discernment, yet we must preserve that child's outlook. Children constantly push their boundaries by trying new things. This is why significant discoveries are often made through child's eyes, pursuing a dream, a profound aspiration, an innate desire. It's also why children learn so quickly.

❖

Albert Einstein's (German physicist, 1879-1955)
words serve as a Life lesson:
"Once you stop learning, you start dying."

***Let's never forget to explore, educate ourselves,
and absorb new information. The key is always
to continue discovering and learning.***

Thus, for years, like Socrates (Greek philosopher, 470-399 BC), I had said to myself: "I know that I know nothing," driving me to progress continually. To embrace Life is devoted to making as many discoveries as possible in the shortest period.

II - MISTAKES

Obviously, stepping into the unknown often leads to misunderstandings or errors in execution.

Nobody likes making mistakes. Mistakes typically lead to further issues that need resolution. Yet, everyone makes them.

As children, we learn from our mistakes through parental guidance, often influenced by the fear of punishment for misdeeds. Hence, if a child stumbles or falls, it's pressing to get back up and try again. As the saying goes, "When you fall off a horse, the best thing to do is to get right back on it."

As we grow older, it's essential to take time to analyze our mistakes rather than escape from them. Similarly, nobody enjoys criticism. Hearing "you did this or that wrong" is uncomfortable. To reduce guilt, we might alter the reality by shifting the blame onto someone else, a neighbor, colleague, spouse, or children.

***However, this behavior only distances us
from the truth and blocks our learning.***

"The real fault is the one that goes uncorrected."
Confucius (Chinese philosopher, 551-479 BC)

To understand and correct our mistakes, we must first acknowledge them. This initial step is the phase of self-reflection. This step is not easy because it involves recognizing and accepting that we can sometimes be foolish, clumsy, stubborn, or mean. We must avoid acting like those who believe they know everything, listen to no one, and always think they are right.

❖

"If you shut the door to all errors, the truth will be shut out."
Rabindranath Tagore (Indian writer, 1861-1941)

*Here lies the importance of being open to the possibility
of being wrong. Doing so makes us more likely
to discover the truth and grow as individuals.*

❖

"What we think we already know often prevents us from learning."
Claude Bernard (French physiologist, 1813-1878)

Our own beliefs and knowledge can block us from learning new information and hinder our progress. Therefore, it's important to be open to new ideas, even if they challenge our existing views on Life.

III - LEARNING

As detailed in the previous section on mistakes, the first step is self-reflection.

The second step is self-development, encompassing learning, change, and improvement. This stage is the longest and most challenging because it involves altering our character traits, personality, thinking processes, and, consequently, our long-established behaviors. The longer we wait, the harder it becomes to change.

It's vital to understand that most of the events we face in Life result from our own actions. In other words, we are responsible, through our actions, for the situations we experience.

❖

If we always perform the same actions,
we will always achieve the same results.

❖

From our thoughts flow our choices. Our choices lead to our actions. Our actions influence the course of our lives. If we want to transform our actions and results, we have to shift the thoughts that created them. Therefore, let's change the way we think, and then change our decisions and actions to achieve unexpected goals.

Also, let's learn to appreciate constructive criticism, which allows us to progress and evolve. Embracing criticism and being open-minded to it are unavoidable steps on the path of personal development.

Constructive criticism serves as a mirror, reflecting areas for improvement and highlighting blind spots we may overlook. By embracing feedback, we open ourselves to valuable insights that can propel us forward, fostering resilience and adaptability.

Moreover, it cultivates humility and a growth mindset, encouraging us to constantly strive for self-improvement. In essence, viewing criticism as a drive for growth transforms setbacks into opportunities for evolution and self-discovery.

❖

*Those who learn the most are
the ones who attempt to rectify their mistakes.*

❖

*Accepting our weaknesses is the first step toward learning.
To accept our weaknesses is to be strong.*

❖

    Denying our weaknesses limits our achievements and prevents us from seizing the new opportunities that would enable us to change the way we look at Life.

    Conversely, accepting our weaknesses frees us to overcome them. We can identify areas for improvement and set goals. We're also more open to receiving help and advice from others, allowing us to be in full possession of our faculties in order to evolve swiftly and thoroughly.

IV - SUCCESS

Life is about making choices and dealing with the consequences. It's essential to believe in our ability to excel, surpass our limitations, and do our best to achieve our goals.

Nevertheless, in this world, there is no such thing as absolute perfection. No one is perfect, and everyone can improve. Being a perfectionist means achieving our primary objective and constantly enhancing the result. It means striving to progress by learning from mistakes and continuously rectifying the process of achieving.

❖

"We should not wait to become perfect to start something good."

"The goal of Life is not the hope of becoming perfect,
it's the desire always to be better."
Ralph Waldo Emerson (American philosopher, 1803-1882)

❖

It's not about achieving absolute perfection but about continuous self-enhancement. Self-improvement enables us to develop new skills and knowledge that help us navigate Life's challenges and opportunities with greater confidence and resilience. Doing so gives us the chance to lead a fulfilling Life.

*Striving for perfection is the best way to interact with,
comprehend, adapt to, and thrive in the world around us.*

❖

*The journey of self-improvement is long and ongoing.
Ultimately, it is a lifelong endeavor.*

Obviously, self-improvement is not easy and can be time-consuming. When faced with a new situation, it is normal to feel fear or tend to retreat. However, like a child, we should approach it head-on, analyze it, understand it, and learn to adapt to it.

"The only real prison is fear.
The only real freedom is to be free from fear."
Aung San Suu Kyi (Burmese, Nobel Peace Prize Laureate 1991)

❖

"We must travel in the direction of our fear."
John Berryman (American poet, 1914-1972)

*The fear of failure often leads us to overthink,
weighing the pros and cons of every situation,
which hinders our progress and blocks our evolution.
We must take the leap.*

❖

This Chinese proverb sums up this idea perfectly:
"Do not fear going slowly. Fear standing still."

❖

Echoing this sentiment, Seneca stated:
"It's not because things are difficult that we dare not venture.
It's because we dare not venture that they are difficult."
Thus, let's not hesitate anymore and take action.

❖

"Try nothing, get nothing," and errors prove you are trying.
"The only man who never makes mistakes
is the man who never does anything."
Theodore Roosevelt (Former US President, 1858-1919)

❖

"Success is walking from failure to failure
while remaining motivated."
Winston Churchill (Former British Prime Minister, 1874-1965)

*Success favors the persistent, the perseverant,
those who never let go and never give up.*

It's also important to note that success isn't always what it seems.
"I never lose; I either win or learn."
Nelson Mandela (First President of South Africa, 1918-2013)

"We learn much more from defeats than from victories."
Carlos Alcaraz (Spanish Tennis Player, 20 years old)

Kilian Jornet, a Spanish athlete, concludes:
"Winning isn't finishing in first place. It isn't beating others. Winning is overcoming oneself. Overcoming our body, our limitations, and our fears. Winning is surpassing oneself and turning dreams into reality."

❖

In essence, the path to success can be envisioned as
a staircase with several steps:

I don't want to do it.
I cannot do it.
I want to do it.
How do I do it?
I will try to do it.
I can do it.
I just do it.
I did it.
This is what success looks like.

Every step in this staircase is fundamental. Looking at the top, the journey might seem long and daunting, which can discourage us. Sometimes, the steps may be uneven or missing and we might even stumble along the way.

"Stay focused on the step in front of you. Nothing else matters."
Bear Grylls (British Special Forces)
Watch your step!

*That's why it's vital to progress steadily,
step by step, to climb up Life's staircase,
because learning to understand Life is
a long, continuous, and never-ending evolution.*

Through the four stages of development – discoveries, mistakes, learning, and successes – we build a dynamic evolution, where each new experience serves as a springboard to new horizons and new perspectives.

Maxime Tarcher, a French psychologist, concludes: "Acquiring new information marks the beginning of a change in our worldview and self-perception."

From knowledge to knowledge, our entire identity transforms.

The knowledge we learn throughout our lives helps us choose, decide, and act. It also allows us to connect with others and form meaningful relationships. Our knowledge shapes our beliefs, values, perspectives, and world understanding. It gives us the capacity to absorb and comprehend it, thus profoundly impacting our identity.

Therefore, it's vital to continuously educate ourselves and, most importantly, maintain a child's outlook on Life because a child's heart is pure and will always be bigger than an adult's heart. This will enable us to keep an open, curious, motivated, and exalted mind, equipping us to handle any situation.

Throughout his Life, my grandpa Charles maintained this child's perspective. Until the end, he marveled at and discovered wonders in this ever-changing world. During his nearly 100-year Lifetime, the world changed and evolved before his eyes.

One last anecdote about him: At 97, he asked my mother to teach him how to use a computer, eager to explore new technologies. How remarkable!

My grandfather taught me how to approach and appreciate this world, to fully savor Life by finding joy in the simplest things.

I now share the letter I wrote him on October 10, 2020,
nine years after his passing.

My beloved Grandfather,
You nurtured me in my childhood.
You taught me to love Life simply: to eat everything, not to waste, to be physically active, to exercise my mind, to be generous with others, to respect, to discover, to joke, and to laugh.
You never had a television or Internet, yet your open-mindedness allowed you to accomplish hundreds of things in your Life. You led such a rich Life filled with experiences until the age of 99.
You left us nine years ago, but you remain present in my heart and mind. And I miss you so dearly. You continue to guide my footsteps every day. Thank you for all you've given me, shaping me into the man I am today. Papi Charles, I love you for Life.

5
EDUCATION

In addition to my grandfather's mentoring, the education my parents provided was meaningful for my personal growth and Live journey. They imparted to me numerous educational principles, which I refer to as the square base. Through its fundamental precepts, I would like to introduce this square base, which is crucial for Life in society.

I - THE SQUARE BASE

My parents' education was grounded in love, respect, sharing, and communication. They provided me with a strict yet necessary and fundamental for my learning.

The term "base" represents the foundations, the bedrock
upon which we rely throughout our lives.

"Square" symbolizes the rigorous rules
that must be followed to progress in Life.

The square base is indispensable.
It's the initial step towards successful education,
proper child development, and societal adaptation.

As Éric Cantona (French artist) put it: "If things aren't square, I go around in circles," meaning that without proper organization, we cannot move forward, trapped in an endless loop.

Parental education is pivotal for a child's intellectual and emotional development. Indeed, to venture into the world and dare to explore, a child must first feel secure and reassured. This sense of security in children is fostered through parental recognition and trust.

For instance, if parents only point out a child's wrongdoings or imply that the child never does enough, the child becomes conditioned to this narrative and may lose self-confidence. Sometimes, this can lead the children never to be satisfied with themselves and develop a tough mindset, always striving to excel. Therefore, parents must strike a delicate balance between criticism and praise.

❖

As Pope John Paul II said:
"Education is more than a profession; it's a mission that involves helping each person to recognize their irreplaceable and unique qualities so they can grow and flourish."

To help is to guide. Guiding means showing the way forward so the individual becomes autonomous, independent, and thus free.

Two simple sentences can symbolize this idea:

❖ "You can't blame the ocean for drowning; you must learn to swim."

❖ "When a man is hungry, it is better to teach him to fish than to give him fish." – Chinese Proverb.

II - FUNDAMENTAL PRECEPTS

From childhood, my parents taught me the basic yet elemental precepts through sayings, quotes, and significant concepts.

**"I must not do to others
what I would not want done to me."**

This is a fundamental principle, an ethic of reciprocity that can be translated as "treat others as you would like to be treated." It's the "Golden Rule" stated in nearly every major religion and culture.

"I must mean what I say."

This means I must be sincere and straightforward, as opposed to hypocritical.
A hypocrite hides their true character, intentions, and feelings behind a facade to present virtues they do not possess in order to gain trust.

"I must do what I say."

This means I must be honest and direct instead of a liar or a fabulist.
A liar or fabulist intentionally obscures the truth, does not provide an accurate reflection of reality, and can mislead.

**"I must turn my tongue seven times
in my mouth before speaking."**

This means we should think carefully before speaking to avoid saying something we might regret later.

Before speaking, we should think:
T - Is it true?
H - Is it helpful?
I - Is it inspiring?
N - Is it necessary?
K - Is it kind?

Furthermore, we should not argue while emotional; we must take time to calm down. Since our actions stem from our thoughts, this reflection time allows us to act with discernment without rushing. In other words, thinking before acting gives us time to make the right decisions and take the best actions.

"The ignorant asserts, the learned doubts, the wise reflects."

This other quote my father taught me about learning, knowledge, and open-mindedness comes from Aristotle (Greek philosopher, 384-322 BC): "The wise keeps silent, the learned listens, the ignorant argues."

This implies that the wise man ponders and does not disclose what they know, the scholar observes and listens to learn, and the ignorant man speaks but does not understand what he says.

When we talk as if we know everything,
we close ourselves to our surroundings.

"Speech is silver, silence is gold." – The Talmud

"Those who know how to speak are not necessarily
the ones with the best things to say."

"It takes two years to learn to speak and
a whole Life to learn to keep quiet."
– Chinese Proverbs –

Trying to converse and communicate with people who always believe they are right is futile because they are closed off and will not listen.

If we overestimate ourselves, thinking we are the best, perfect, and superior to others, we cannot listen, and thus, we freeze and do not evolve. Constant self-introspection is necessary to be aware of our strengths and weaknesses.

"Knowing one's ignorance is the best part of knowledge."
Lao Zi (Chinese Philosopher, 500 BC)

We can learn much more when we listen, observe, and think than when we speak. If we talk, we can hear but not listen to what people say or want to convey.

Note a significant difference between hearing and listening. According to their definitions:

- ❖ Hearing is a physical ability; only the ear allows us to perceive sound.

- ❖ Listening is a so-called cognitive ability linked to the brain, allowing us to understand the meaning of a statement or question. Listening requires attention and concentration.

For good learning and good instruction, listening is, therefore, much more essential than hearing. Likewise, don't just look, observe. Observation and listening are two crucial skills for rapid learning.

❖

"The Four Agreements"

"The Four Agreements" is a book published in 1997 by Mexican author Miguel Ruiz. Translated into 52 languages and with 20 million copies sold, it is the most purchased book of wisdom globally.

This book has become a touchstone in personal development, wherein the author shares fundamental Life principles:

- ❖ Let your words be impeccable by using your speech wisely.
- ❖ Whatever happens, don't take it personally, and do not internalize others' actions or words.
- ❖ Don't make assumptions and avoid asserting unverified hypotheses.
- ❖ Always do your best.

Since 2020, a fifth agreement has been added:

- ❖ Be skeptical, yet learn to listen. You can question but remain open to opinions different from yours.

❖

❖

I now share a note distributed by teachers to students' parents, encompassing all the learning rules.

We remind parents that it is at home
where their child should learn the magic words:

- ❖ Good morning
- ❖ Good evening
- ❖ Please
- ❖ May I
- ❖ Excuse me
- ❖ Thank you so much

It is also at home where they must learn:

- ❖ To be honest
- ❖ Not to lie
- ❖ To be appropriate
- ❖ To be punctual
- ❖ Not to say bad words
- ❖ To show solidarity
- ❖ To respect friends, older people, and teachers
- ❖ To be hygiene
- ❖ Not to speak with a full mouth
- ❖ Not to litter
- ❖ To be organized
- ❖ To take care of personal belongings
- ❖ Not to steal

The professors concluded by saying:
"Please spread this message; it is for the good of our nation."

❖

❖

However, the quote that has been with me since my childhood, profoundly impacting me, is from Antoine de Saint-Exupéry (French writer, 1900-1944) in the book "The Little Prince":

**"We see clearly only with the heart.
What is essential is invisible to the eyes."**

As perfectly explained by "French Expressions," ("Expressions Françaises") this quote reminds me that:

❖ I must learn to look beyond appearances and focus on what truly matters, not the superficial.

❖ I must open up to others and give them a chance because I never know what I could learn from them.

❖ I must also open up to myself and accept myself as I am.

❖ I must appreciate the small things in Life and be grateful for what I have.

❖ I must also stop and take the time to enjoy simple moments and the beauty around me.

This quote is a precious Life lesson, a reminder for all humanity.

❖

❖

With my parents, I received a very rigorous but fair upbringing. In my childhood, I faced difficult times like all families, but looking back, I repeatedly thanked my parents for the education they provided me. It still guides my footsteps and has allowed me to adapt to many situations.

Ultimately, parental education is paramount for children's proper development. It lays the fundamental groundwork that will guide them throughout their lives.

In summary, one must strive to be happy every day, laugh a lot, respect one another, be polite, say kind words, always tell the truth, keep promises, and be grateful.

6
ILLNESS AND HEALING

I was always a healthy and energetic boy, however, at the age of 12, I developed a severe illness. During this painful period, I completely changed my outlook on Life. It was one of my most unforgettable experiences, and it burst my love for Life.

The illness began with severe fatigue, followed by the appearance of numerous red and purple marks all over my body. After a few days, I started experiencing nosebleeds that wouldn't stop, prompting my parents to take me to the hospital. Blood tests revealed that I had contracted a severe blood disorder known as thrombocytopenia.

This condition relates to the blood cells in the body, specifically the platelets, known as thrombocytes. Platelets, produced in the bone marrow, are essential for blood clotting and tissue healing, helping to stop bleeding. They play an irreplaceable role in the body.

Thrombocytopenia leads to a reduced number of platelets in the blood, causing symptoms like nosebleeds, bruising, and, in worst cases, intestinal or cerebral hemorrhages that can cause the removal of the spleen or even be fatal.

In my case, the disease was triggered by an autoimmune reaction to the antibiotic penicillin, leading to "idiopathic thrombocytopenic purpura," one of the most severe forms. In my condition, my immune system produced antibodies against my platelets, causing their destruction and disappearance in large numbers.

Normally, the average platelet count ranges between 150,000 and 300,000 per cubic millimeter of blood. However, in my worst situation, the platelets were almost untraceable, with a count of 7,000 per cubic millimeter of blood.

Immediately, I was admitted to the intensive care unit. Having lost a significant amount of blood, I began receiving blood transfusions. Throughout my hospital stay, I was bedridden with continuous infusions – blood transfusions through the veins in my left hand and glucose transfusions in my right hand.

Moreover, I was also on a specific no-salt diet. Due to my advanced state of fatigue, I could only move in a wheelchair to the bathroom two or three times a week, and obviously, I had a urinal by my bed.

Every day, I underwent multiple blood tests to monitor the disease's progression. I remember having needle marks all over my arms. I had so many blood tests that the doctor didn't even know which veins to choose, though I got used to the injections.

But the needles were nothing compared to the bone marrow biopsies; it was unbearable, especially in the hip bone without any anesthesia. Nothing could ease the pain. To this day, I can still feel the needle penetrating my bones.

Unfortunately, in my case, allopathic medicine has no treatment to regulate the immune system. The doctors could do nothing to reverse the process; just wait for a natural progression.

Yet, I didn't lose hope. After countless blood tests and bone penetrations, somewhat miraculously, to the medical staff's astonishment, my blood levels gradually normalized, and eventually, I was discharged from the hospital.

❖

After two months of lying still and sitting in a wheelchair, I couldn't walk much due to muscle atrophy. But that couldn't take me down, as I was just happy to have a normal Life again. More importantly, after what I went through, minor injuries or pains could never bother me again.

Since that day, whenever I see someone disabled, in a wheelchair, or on crutches, I feel great compassion and thank Life for having a resilient body and remaining in good health.

Ever since this experience has constantly reminded me how fortunate I am to be just alive, and it has instilled in me a desire to appreciate Life even more, valuing it to its fullest.

7
SCHOOL AND STUDIES

Through my personal experiences and academic journey, I will explore the significance of school and studies.

Let me pose a question first:
"What is the difference between school and Life?"

I - SCHOOL

Parental education is the initial step in a child's learning process and is paramount for their proper development. Nonetheless, the education received at school has equal importance.

By teaching mathematics, science, geography, history, languages, and literature, the school provides us with the knowledge and general culture we need to pursue higher education, acquire a trade, or enter the world of work. It also plays a role in socialization and learning about Life in the community.

Teachers could, in fact, support parents in the education they provide at home. Passing on knowledge, whatever the field, is one of the most beautiful and most difficult vocations. It is an honourable mission that enables students to grow and develop.

Unfortunately, however, teachers have lost much of their authority over their students, and this is causing problems in some schools. This interferes with their lessons and the transmission of their knowledge. Nevertheless, let's not forget that teachers are heroes.

❖

On the other hand, bullying and violence are becoming more and more common in schools. A note to all students. If you see:

- ❖ A student struggling to make friends.
- ❖ A student being bullied.
- ❖ A student who is new or shy, or doesn't fit in with the crowd.
- ❖ A student eating alone.

Be friendly. Be integrators. Be connectors. Be leaders.

Say hi or smile. Ask if you can sit together. Speak and share. A small gesture could mean much more. We never know what that person might be dealing with inside or outside school.

Something we might not realize until we stop studying is how school is a crucial stage of Life. It provides foundational knowledge and helps us develop communication, critical thinking, problem-solving, and teamwork skills. These skills are essential for success in the professional world, regardless of the field we choose.

In conclusion, school and studies equip us with the necessary knowledge to understand the world and make the right decisions. Thus, it's vital to be engaged, work diligently, and show respect for teachers and fellow students.

II - UNIFORM

It is important to note that most countries use a uniform or united outfit at school. In the United States, uniforms are making a comeback to combat gang affiliation. In Europe, only some countries use uniforms. (Source: Wikipedia)

Nations that have refused or abandoned uniforms, view them as outdated or a restriction of freedoms, which I consider to be a mistake.

However, the uniform or united outfit offers excellent benefits:

- ❖ It prevents fashion-based discrimination.
- ❖ It erases social inequalities between the wealthy and the poor.
- ❖ It supports secularism by avoiding signs of religious or political affiliation.
- ❖ It creates a homogeneous group without distinctions, fostering companionship.
- ❖ It structures students by imposing a model, guiding them to respect rules and authority.
- ❖ It also saves time when dressing and often saves money.

Ultimately, uniforms promote community Life, self-discipline, and order in educational institutions. In countries where uniforms are used, like Japan, education and culture are highly respected.

Adopting the uniforms offers many advantages.

III - ACADEMIC BACKGROUND

1 - Elementary and Middle School

I grew up in Nice. My first kindergarten was at the Magnolias School from 1982 to 1984. Then, I attended elementary school at Corniche Fleurie School, where I stayed from 1985 to 1990. Subsequently, I moved on to Raoul Dufy Middle School in 1991, where I passed the middle school certificate in 1994.

2 - High School

Starting high school, my parents decided to enroll me in a boarding school in Grasse, at the Fénelon Institute, a rather strict private school. Initially, I was reluctant to go because it was in a different city, an unfamiliar place, away from my family and friends. However, I ended up staying there for three years, from 1994 to 1997, and by the end, I didn't want to leave.

At this school, I lived 24/7, five days a week, with about a hundred other students from various cities. I made many lasting friendships with whom I am still in contact.
This institution truly taught me about community living. We were all brothers, like one big family. We shared rooms, studied together, dined in the cafeteria, and helped and supported each other in any situation. It made me realize that having true friends is like having a second family.

After that, I experienced public education at Beau Site High School, right next to Honoré d'Estienne d'Orves High School, in 1997 in Nice. There, I reunited with middle school friends and made many new acquaintances among students from both high schools. I graduated with a scientific baccalaureate in 1999.

3 - First job

Parallel to my studies, I earned the BAFA certificate, a qualification for youth leaders in holiday centers and leisure camps. This certification allows to supervise children aged 6 to 12 during weekends or school holidays in centers where parents leave their children for some free time.

For two years, I had looked after children during the holidays, offering a range of physical, sportive, educational, intellectual, and social activities.

I always preferred the company of children to adults because their open-mindedness is boundless. They are curious, intrigued, always motivated, and, above all, full of positive energy. I loved being around them because they brought me good feelings. I admired their outlook on Life, and their pure, healthy energies rejuvenated me. It also enabled me to earn my first wages.

70 years after my grandfather, I also obtained my Pediatric Basic Life Support (PBLS) certificate, which includes the first aid techniques adapted to children and babies.

4 - Universities

After I passed my baccalaureate,
two Chinese quotes resonated with me:

- ❖ "If you don't study when you are young, you will regret the time wasted when you are old."
- ❖ "He who asks a question is a fool for five minutes; he who does not ask a question remains a fool forever."

Thus, I pursued studies at various universities in Nice Sophia-Antipolis to find my path. I attended the Faculty of Sports from 1999-2000, the Faculty of Medicine from 2000-2001, and the Faculty of Letters from 2001-2003.

I earned a university diploma from the Faculty of Letters on "The principle of health and well-being in traditional Chinese thought."

Ultimately, I enrolled in the Faculty of Psychology at the Saint-Jean d'Angely campus, where I stayed for four years. I obtained a university degree in psychology.

My years at university were instrumental in broadening my general knowledge, enhancing my understanding of various fields, exploring new horizons, and meeting new people.

❖

As Seneca wisely stated:
"Study, not to know more, but to know better."

❖

Psychology is the science of human behavior and mental processes. It delves into how people think, feel, and act. We all experience emotional variations, and thus psychological ones. It becomes pathological when our maladaptive behaviors are recurrent, constant, and uncontrollable.

The courses I took in psychology allowed me to put scientific words to my emotions, understand the genesis of my behaviors, and consequently, learn to know myself better.

Psychology is based on understanding oneself to interpret better, analyze, and control one's emotions, in order to have the openness to understand others.

❖

*We can only deeply understand others
once we have understood ourselves.*

❖

This implies that self-understanding is precedential for comprehending others. With it, we can decode and assimilate external elements and situations.

❖

It's worth noting that psychology occurs every moment of Life through numerous daily activities:

- ❖ In our relationships with others: Psychology aids us in understanding others' behaviors and improving our communication with them.

- ❖ In our work: It helps us better understand our motivations, develop skills, and manage stress.

- ❖ In our health: It assists us in preventing and treating mental disorders.

- ❖ In our personal lives: It enables us to comprehend our intimate relationships better, make the right decisions, and manage our emotions.

This approach applies to everyone in any daily Life situation.

5 - Conclusion

In sum, as French actor Albert Dupontel once told a friend of mine, "Just because you're a dunce at school doesn't mean you'll be a dunce in Life." Because it's not a school exam that defines us but what we do with our lives. I have friends who didn't pursue extensive academic studies yet have succeeded marvelously in Life.

One day, years after finishing my studies, I told my father, "You know, I didn't learn to be a psychologist in the university; I learned to be a psychologist little by little, through every single person I've met in every single day of my Life."

❖

Life is my school.
Through Life, I learn every moment.

❖

"Knowledge is acquired through experience,
Everything else is just information."
– Albert Einstein –

Let's try not to limit our studies to a single field, and let's not hesitate to diversify our knowledge. We must embrace all the possibilities available to us for learning and growth. Accepting differences allows our minds to learn, discover, store, and fully emancipate.

Learning is crucial for advancement and progress, not just in school or university but also in Life. The knowledge I've accumulated will serve me well in my future endeavors.

❖

To conclude, I answer the question:
"What is the difference between school and Life?"

"The school teaches us lessons and then gives us a test.
Life gives us a test, and then we learn the lessons."

8
SPORT

In all the activities I've engaged in, sports have held a significant place. Sports make us live younger, longer, and healthier, but more importantly, they make us tougher in mind, allow us to keep fighting until the end, and never give up. Through various testimonials from professionals in the sports world and my athletic journey, I would like to present all the benefits of sports.

At six, I dreamt of becoming a soccer player like many boys. However, I practiced various sports in clubs, such as tennis, handball, table tennis, volleyball, athletics, baseball, sailing, French boxing, and rock climbing. Yet, alongside these, I could always find time for football, playing at school or with friends.

From a young age, I loved watching most sporting events, including the Olympic Games, Grand Slam tennis tournaments, Formula 1 World Championships, rally championships, and team sports matches, with a particular fondness for football.

Regardless of the sport we're interested in or the team we support, sports provide beneficial and positive emotions for both body and mind, whether actively participating or simply watching.

Sports offer advantages and develop
numerous virtues in us that few other fields can.

❖

Pierre de Coubertin (French, 1863-1937), founder of the International Olympic Committee and creator of the Olympic rings, epitomizes these qualities with the three values of Olympism: Excellence, Friendship, and Respect.

In 1894, he established the Olympic motto,
inspired by Father Henri Didon (French, 1840-1900):
"Citius - Altius - Fortius," which means
"Faster - higher - stronger."

- ❖ The Olympic motto promotes the value of excellence, encouraging athletes to always surpass themselves.
- ❖ The Olympic flame, relayed through numerous countries worldwide, symbolizes friendship among people.
- ❖ The Olympic rings represent respect, uniting all nations and continents in peace without discrimination.

Pierre de Coubertin adds: "Let us remember, gentlemen, these strong words: the important thing in Life is not the triumph, but the fight, it is not to have won, but to have fought well" inspired by the American bishop Ethelbert Talbot (1848-1928):

"The important thing is to participate."

A few quotes perfectly embody the values of sports:

- ❖ "Sport involves delegating to the body some of the soul's greatest virtues: energy, daring, and patience." – Jean Giraudoux (French writer, 1882-1944)

- ❖ "Giving, receiving, sharing. These fundamental virtues of the athletes are timeless and universal. They are sports." "Sport is about surpassing oneself. Sport is a school of Life." – Aimé Jacquet (French football coach and 1998 World Cup winner)

- ❖ "In sports, as in Life, you need to be focused and relaxed, not distracted and tense" – Bernard Tapie (French former president of Olympique de Marseille, 1943-2021)

❖ "Sport, like rock'n'roll, is a dominant cultural force, speaks an international language, and both are about emotion." – Philip Knight (American CEO)

❖ "Football, like all sports, is a game, a pleasure, a happiness generator capable of bringing people together and uniting them." – Didier Drogba (Ivorian soccer player)

Sport is a universal language that brings out profound emotional reactions.

Returning to my sporting experiences, as the son of a Franco-Italian mother and a father from Marseille, I was ultimately born in Nice, making me the 8th generation of "Niçois." A flood of emotions was already flowing through my veins.

Since childhood, as a huge sports fan, all kinds of emotions swept over me when I watched a live sports match: I got chills singing the national anthem, felt anxious before a decisive move, disappointed after a missed opportunity, perplexed by an overturned call, scream with joy after a goal, immersed in an indescribable euphoria following a victory, and then running around in all directions. These emotions are still inside me today.

As an enthusiastic football fan, I've been to the Vélodrome Stadium in Marseille several times, experiencing its incredible atmosphere. However, I more frequently attended matches at the Ray Stadium in the heart of Nice or the Louis II Stadium in Monaco, which felt like home. Sadly, the Ray Stadium was demolished in 2016 to make way for the Allianz Riviera, taking with it many emotions and memories of the past.

The matches between Nice and Marseille, two neighboring cities, were always particularly special to me. Caught between my birth city and my heart city, I generally rooted for the best team to win, though a draw was perfectly satisfactory.

In 1993, during Olympique de Marseille soccer club's Champions League triumph against the formidable AC Milan, I was 14 years old, but such emotions are imprinted on me forever. Years later, I had the immense joy and privilege of meeting Mr. Basile Boli, the scorer of the winning goal in the Champions League final, securing Olympique de Marseille's victory. He is a soccer legend.

Additionally, Dom, one of my best friends, was the maître d'hôtel on the Phocea, Bernard Tapie's yacht, allowing me to see the pennant from the 1993 final. The pennant, a small flag representing the sporting event, is produced in just three copies. I held the one given to the winning President, which made me relive that particular moment again. What a sensation!

The only Marseille jersey I own is the gold one created for the 1998/1999 season, commemorating the club's centennial. The jersey is emblazoned with "Fabrizio Ravanelli," a famous Italian soccer player.

❖

To conclude, I share a thought from Mats Wilander (Swedish tennis player) about Yannick Noah (French tennis player) after the Roland Garros Grand Slam final won by Noah in 1983:
"He was different from how Life had been presented to me until then. He wasn't a tennis player. In my eyes, he was a human being larger than Life. Normally, you don't meet such people. That's why, as the match went on, I cared less and less about winning." Nothing but respect for that!

Yannick Noah added:
"The worst thing is not even dreaming of winning."

❖

❖

In short, sports bring natural sensations, healthy excitement, and pure emotions. This activity releases the most endorphin molecules in our body, responsible for the sensation of well-being. Thus, sports are the best activity for maintaining good mental and physical health.

Sports free our minds.
Sports are raw happiness.

Sports positively impact every part of our body, just like laughter. As mentioned in Chapter 2, my grandfathers engaged in extensive physical activities, allowing them to live long lives, up to 95 and 99 years old.

So, let's take action and engage in sports.

❖

I'll end by saying, "Allez l'OM and Issa Nissa," the rallying cries of Marseille and Nice football fans to support their teams and display their pride in being supporters.

But no matter the team we support or the sport we play, remember that we must always respect our opponents, accept our defeat, and be an elegant winner, after all, sports are just games, and we should live them with passion but, more importantly, without violence.

9
SCOUTS

To expose me to new experiences, my parents enrolled me in the Scouts of France and later in the Scouts of Europe. My experiences with Scouts were enlightening and immensely prepared me for the rest of my Life. The foundations it teaches could apply to all of humanity. Through its history, its benefits, and my experiments, I will describe this global movement.

1 - Introduction

Robert Baden-Powell (former British Army officer, 1857-1941) founded Scouting in 1907 in England with the "Boys Scouts." He laid out its foundations in his first book, "Scouting for Boys," published in 1908, followed by a second volume. In total, he authored around forty books. (Source: Wikipedia)

The Scouts of France were established in 1920 and remained active until 2004, when they merged with the Guides of France, primarily based in France. The Scouts of Europe were founded in 1958 and held gatherings across all European countries.

Today, scouting boasts over 40 million members across 217 countries and territories, in color on the map, encompassing all religions and nationalities.

It's a worldwide youth movement based on learning values such as solidarity, teamwork, mutual support, and respect, and often has a religious or spiritual dimension.

Furthermore, it aims to help young individuals form their character and build their personality while contributing to their physical, mental, and spiritual development.

Scouting is structured around a Promise, a salute, a Law, an emblem, a logo, a motto, a uniform, badges, survival gear, and activities created by Robert Baden-Powell.

2 - The Scout Promise

The Scout Promise is a solemn commitment made by the youth during a ceremony to mark their adherence to the law and values of the Scout movement they've joined.

It goes: "On my honor, I promise to do my best to fulfill my duties to God and the King, to help other people at all times, to contribute to a better world, and to obey the Scout Law."

3 - The Scout salute

The Scout Salute, performed for the first time during the Promise, is a hand sign where the index, middle, and ring fingers are vertical, straight, and together, while the thumb is bent over the little finger. This sign represents loyalty, protection of the weaker, aid to others, and respect for the Scout Law.

4 - The Scout Law

The Scout Law is a set of Life guidelines in ten articles, fundamental for living appropriately in community and society.

It states:

- ❖ A Scout's honor is to be trusted.
- ❖ A Scout is loyal to the king, officers, parents, employers, and employees.
- ❖ A Scout's duty is to be useful and help others.
- ❖ A Scout is the friend and brother of all scouts, whatever social class they belong to.
- ❖ A Scout is courteous.
- ❖ A Scout is a friend of animals.
- ❖ A Scout obeys the orders of his parents, patrol leader, or instructor without question.
- ❖ A Scout smiles and whistles when he encounters difficulty.
- ❖ A Scout is thrifty.
- ❖ A Scout is pure in his thoughts, words, and actions.

5 - The Scout emblem

The world Scout emblem encompasses these elements.

- ❖ White symbolizes purity.
- ❖ Purple represents leadership.
- ❖ The two stars stand for truth and knowledge.
- ❖ The ten points of the stars represent the ten parts of the Scout Law.
- ❖ The left side of the fleur-de-lis symbolizes duty to our country and service to others.
- ❖ The right side of the fleur-de-lis represents duty to oneself and obedience to the Scout Law.
- ❖ The bond at the base of the fleur-de-lis represents the Scout family.
- ❖ The rope encircling symbolizes the unity of the Scout movement worldwide.
- ❖ The knot signifies the strength of the global Scout movement.
- ❖ The compass needle at the center of the fleur-de-lis signifies always showing the right way.
- ❖ The tip symbolizes duty to God and Scout's values.

6 - The uniform

The Scout uniform typically consists of a shirt paired with a neckerchief, with colors varying by age and region.

For the Scouts and Guides of France, uniform colors are:
6 to 8 years old, light green. 8 to 11 years old, yellow or orange.
11 to 14 years old, blue. 14 to 17 years old, red.
17 to 21 years old, dark green.

For the Scouts of Europe, the uniform color is consistent across all ages, often accompanied by a cap or beret.

7 - The badges

Scout shirts are adorned with various badges indicating the company name, territory, role, Scout Promise, Scout logo, affiliation, and country.

8 - Equipment

A Scout must always carry survival gear for solitary nature expeditions, including:
- ❖ A torch for getting around at night.
- ❖ Rope to build a shelter.
- ❖ A compass to orient ourselves.
- ❖ A knife for cutting rope or wood.
- ❖ A Swiss army knife is very useful in all situations.
- ❖ A bottle to collect water.
- ❖ A shovel to dig and build foundations.

9 - Activities

Scouting involves numerous practical activities in nature and the forest, teaching skills to:
- ❖ Set up a tent.
- ❖ Make fire.
- ❖ Cook and eat in the forest.
- ❖ Build shelters.
- ❖ Make knots is very useful for wooden constructions.
- ❖ Study plants.
- ❖ Orient ourselves with a compass and maps.
- ❖ Make discoveries.
- ❖ Protect the environment.
- ❖ Have fun and have good times with friends.

The Scouts use only natural and biodegradable materials, mainly wood and plants, to build their camp, consisting of a shelter, a kitchen, a sleeping area, and toilets.

10 - The Scout logo and motto

The Scout motto, represented on the logo, is "BE PREPARED," signified "BE READY," which, over the years, evolved to "Scout always ready."

Same as in Life, we must always be ready in our body and mind to do our duty. We must always be prepared to face any challenges that might arise.

Two quotes illustrate this idea well.

"A problem without a solution is a poorly stated problem."
– Albert Einstein –

"There are no problems; there are only solutions."
André Gide (French writer, 1869-1951)

❖

Each morning,
I wake up with more solutions than problems.

❖

Scouting taught me to live harmoniously with nature, develop survival instincts, and adapt to unpredictable situations.

As Bear Grylls declared: "The attraction of nature for me lies in its unpredictability. You must develop awareness, respond quickly, be resourceful, make a plan, and act accordingly."

I am a huge fan of "Man vs. Wild," where Bear Grylls demonstrates how to adapt and survive in a wild, hostile, desert, or icy environment. He teaches us how to find the four primal factors for "Survival": locating clean and potable water, finding edible food, making a fire to cook, keeping warm and preventing wild animals, and finding shelter to sleep safely.

Sometimes, Bear Grylls's methods are extreme, such as drinking muddy water, making fire in the snow, or sleeping in the jungle in a hammock made from lianas.

He might consume unconventional food like scorpions, larvae, or snakes, emphasizing the importance of finding nutritious food to sustain Life. I particularly enjoy when he describes the horrible taste of these foods, explaining: "It's disgusting, but it's good for my body; it's full of vitamins and proteins," and always with a mischievous smile and a childlike sparkle in his eyes.

Bear Grills concludes by saying: "Adventure should be a part of everyone's Life. It's the difference between being fully alive and simply existing."

11 - Conclusion

I never served in the military; I was part of the cohort when military service was reformed in France from a year to just three days in 1996, and thus, I was exempted.

However, my scouting experiences were incredibly enriching, teaching me self-discipline, respect for authority, and community living. Scout implanted in me social values, adaptability, and appreciation towards nature, proving invaluable throughout my Life. With these lessons, I was prepared for Life's upcoming challenges.

One day, someone asked me:
"How would you define intelligence in one word?"
I responded instantly: ***"Intelligence is adaptation."***

For me, intelligence is our ability to adapt to all the situations we may encounter throughout Life. Intelligence is our capacity to solve problems efficiently. Intelligence is adapting our body and mind as quickly as possible to the world around us.

❖

With all these experiences, like the Scout motto:
I am ready always to be ready.

❖

Just before his death, in his farewell letter to all Scouts,
Robert Baden-Powell wrote:

"Always be faithful to your Scout Promise even when
you are no longer a child, and may God help you to achieve it!"

10
TIME IS LIFE

My grandpa Charles, to celebrate his 95th birthday, wrote a text which sums up Life:

"Admit it to yourself and say it aloud, not to see your friends protest but to confirm your tastes and forbid yourself from doing what you thought you were capable/allowed just the day before.

With serenity, as soon as dawn rises, we can convince ourselves that we are a day older. To each white hair parting with a dream and whispering to them an unreturnable farewell.

On gluttony imposed true fasts and nourished one's mind with strong knowledge. Become good and become gentle.

Love young people as we love flowers, as we love hope. Resign yourself to live a little on the shore while they sail on the hazardous waves.

Afraid of being important without becoming wild. Allowing oneself to be ignored while remaining close to them. Handle quietly with the care that every departure requires, pray, and do a little good around you. Also, do not neglect one's body and soul.

Then, one fine evening, discreetly blow out the flame from one's tongue and die because it's the law of Life.

Almost a century and I'm still here, 34698 days. A busy Life with ups and downs. Fruitful days, though too short with Madeleine, surrounded by our children. My Life continues to be illuminated by this whole big family.

What matters most in Life is taking the children by the hand until the day we can tiptoe away. It is what I am going to do."

❖

THE FLAME

"The candle flame is like a human being; it lives and dies. Its Life is fiery and impetuous. As long as it lasts, it dances, leaps, and appears to live without a care in the world.

Although it may be joyful, it meets a tragic end. The tragedy lies in its struggle not to die. Initially, it emits an eerie bluish magnetic/enchanting glow, and just before it goes out, it flickers, jumps, and starts living again.

Then, it seems like its vital momentum to survive would be victorious, the flame crackles, extending itself as if clinging to the fate that threatens it, but to no avail. Neither the flame nor the human is destined for eternal Life."

– My friend Nadya –

TIME

There's only one way to embrace it fully,
by remembering what really matters.

Certainly, keeping sight of what's important can be difficult. What matters is not necessarily other people's expectations. It's not that easy, but we shouldn't have to worry about it.

In a way, it feels like we'll always be alone, and the only thing that keeps us company are our own thoughts and doubts. When difficulties arise, we tell ourselves that we are the problem, especially when uncontrollable situations come our way.

That's why we need to forget the doubts, sorrows, egos, resents, and pains and remember what we are really fighting for, what we live for: the people who matter in our lives, the people we love. (Inspired by "The Last Airbender")

We ought to live for ourselves, take care of our loved ones while respecting the world around us and adapting to the flow of Life. It's time to take action and make the world a better place. Let this be the light that guides us through the darkest night and the most perilous times.

*Only after understanding these principles with heart,
we could live a fulfilled and happy Life.*

11
EPILOGUE

The knowledge and experience I have accumulated during the first steps of my Life will accompany me and serve as a guide throughout my journey.

Because everything that happens to us in Life is part of our existence. We all have our ups and downs, but in the end, from the day we were born until today, it is nothing other than a straight line, curved or sinusoidal, but continuous, that makes us the beings we are.

Throughout our existence, we plant several seeds. Some seeds die, others sprout without growing much, and then some, with Time, patience, care, hard work, and maintenance, might become great majestic trees. This is what Life is all about.

So, like my grandpa Charles, let's never stop approaching Life with wonder, finding joy in the simplest moments, and discovering the inexhaustible treasures of this world, because no matter how much we learn, there's always more to explore and understand.

The key is to be in action and to plant our own seeds, even if we don't know where they will lead. The essential thing is to devote time to cultivating deep roots and building solid foundations, which become the bedrock for our evolution and fulfillment.

Let's take inspiration from my grandfather's vision and the wisdom of his extraordinary journey to live a Life filled with love, respect, sharing, passion, humor, joy, and an unshakeable desire for discovery.

❖

*Let's always remember that Time is Life.
So let's take the Time to seize the Time
and let's hasten to fully enjoy Life
in Respect and Peace.*

*I'm just an open door pointing a way.
If people can take one step on that path,
I'll be happy.*

TO BE CONTINUED...

www.ingramcontent.com/pod-product-compliance
Lightning Source LLC
Chambersburg PA
CBHW060404050426
42449CB00009B/1896